THE BIG BOOK OF AUS...

AN EDUCATIONAL COUNTRY TRAVEL PICTURE BOOK FOR KIDS ABOUT HISTORY, DESTINATION PLACES, ANIMALS AND MANY MORE

GW01312056

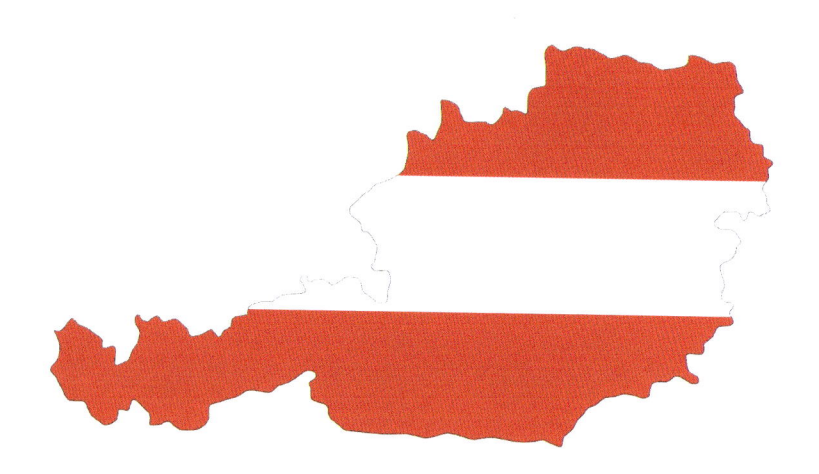

Copyright @2023 James K. Mahi

Austria is a country located in central Europe.

Austria's population is approximately 9.1 million people.

the national bird of Austria is the **barn swallow**

the national animal of Austria is the **black eagle.**

the national sport of Austria is **skiing.**

the national tree of Austria is the **silver fir.**

What is the official name of Austria?

The official name of Austria is the Republic of Austria.

What are the people of Austria called?

The people of Austria are called Austrians.

How big is Austria?

Austria has a total area of approximately 83,879 square kilometers (32,386 square miles).

Which city is the largest in Austria?

Vienna is the largest city in Austria, with a population of around 1.9 million people in the metropolitan area.

Is Austria overly populated?

No, Austria is not considered overly populated. the estimated population of Austria was around 9.1 million people, with a population density of approximately 106 people per square kilometer (275 people per square mile).

How many states does Austria have?

Austria is divided into nine states, including Vienna, Lower Austria, Upper Austria, Styria, Tyrol, Carinthia, Salzburg, Burgenland, and Vorarlberg.

How much of Austria is covered by rainforests?

Austria does not have any rainforests. The country is primarily covered by forests, grasslands, and mountains.

How much of the world's land Austria takes up?

Austria has a total area of approximately 83,879 square kilometers (32,386 square miles), which makes up about 0.058% of the world's total land area.

How many time zones are there in Austria?

Austria is in a single time zone, which is Central European Time (CET), also known as GMT+1.

What is the highest temperature recorded in Austria?

The highest temperature ever recorded in Austria was 40.5°C (104.9°F) in August 2013 in the town of Bad Deutsch-Altenburg.

What is the coldest temperature recorded in Austria?

The coldest temperature ever recorded in Austria was −52.6°C (−62.7°F) in January 2002 in the town of Lienz.

Which months are the coldest in Austria?

The coldest months in Austria are typically January and February, while the hottest months are typically July and August.

Which months are the hottest in Austria?

The hottest months in Austria are generally July and August, with average high temperatures ranging from 25°C to 30°C (77°F to 86°F). However, temperatures can vary depending on the region and altitude.

What is the old name of Austria?

The old name of Austria was Ostarrichi, which dates back to the 10th century. It was later known as the Duchy of Austria and then the Austrian Empire before becoming the Republic of Austria in 1919.

The official language of Austria is German.

- The currency used in Austria is the Euro.
- Austria is one of the richest countries in the world and has a high standard of living. It has a strong economy based on services, manufacturing, and tourism
- Austria is famous for its beautiful scenery, cultural events, and ski resorts, which attract many tourists from around the world. Tourism is a major source of income for Austria

Vienna is the capital and largest city of Austria.

Austria is known for its beautiful mountains, lakes and forests.

- The Austrian Alps are some of the highest and most famous mountains in Europe.
- The Austrian Alps cover around 62% of Austria's total area and are part of the Central Eastern Alps, which comprise the main chain of the Eastern Alps
- The highest peak in the Austrian Alps is Grossglockner, which is 3,798 meters (12,461 feet) tall.

The Danube River runs through Austria, and is an important transportation route for the country.

Austria is home to many famous composers, including Wolfgang Amadeus Mozart and Johann Strauss Jr.

Austria is famous for its ski resorts, which attract visitors from all over the world.

Austria is also known for its delicious food, including Wiener schnitzel, apfelstrudel, and sachertorte.

Coffeehouses are an important part of Austrian culture, and are a great place to relax and enjoy a cup of coffee and a pastry.

The Habsburg dynasty, one of the most important royal families in Europe, originated in Austria.

The Schönbrunn Palace, also in Vienna, is one of the most famous and beautiful palaces in the world.

Austria has a long history of producing world-class athletes, especially in skiing and ice hockey.

The Vienna State Opera is one of the most famous opera houses in the world.

The Spanish Riding School in Vienna is famous for its beautiful Lipizzaner horses and classical dressage performances.

The Salzburg Festival is a world–renowned music and theatre festival that takes place every summer in Salzburg, Austria.

The Salzkammergut region of Austria is known for its stunning lakes and mountains, and is a popular destination for tourists.

The city of Innsbruck, located in the Austrian Alps, has hosted the Winter Olympics twice.

The Vienna Zoo is the oldest and one of the best zoos in the world.

The Mauthausen Concentration Camp, located near Linz, Austria, is a sobering reminder of the horrors of the Holocaust.

The Wiener Riesenrad, a giant Ferris wheel located in Vienna, is a popular tourist attraction.

The Melk Abbey, located in the Wachau Valley, is a beautiful baroque monastery and a UNESCO World Heritage Site.

- The Austrian flag is red and white, and has been used since 1230.
- The Austrian flag is one of the oldest national flags in the world, and has been in use since 1230.

The Grossglockner High Alpine Road is one of the most scenic drives in Europe, and offers stunning views of the Austrian Alps.

The Salzburg Cathedral, located in the heart of Salzburg, is a beautiful example of baroque architecture.

The Austrian National Library, located in Vienna, contains over 7.4 million items, including rare books, manuscripts, and maps.

The Vienna U–Bahn, or subway system, is one of the most efficient and modern in the world.

The Hohensalzburg Fortress, located in Salzburg, is one of the largest medieval castles in Europe.

The Zillertal Valley, located in the Austrian Alps, is a popular destination for skiing and snowboarding.

The Salzburger Nockerl, a sweet soufflé dessert, is a traditional Austrian dish.

The Semmering Railway, a historic railway line that connects Vienna with the Austrian Alps, is a UNESCO World Heritage Site.

The Austrian National Day is celebrated on October 26th each year.

The Wachau Valley, located along the Danube River, is a UNESCO World Heritage Site known for its stunning scenery and vineyards.

20 TRAVEL TIPS FOR TOURISTS VISITING AUSTRIA

- **Taste the local food:** Austrian dishes like Wiener Schnitzel and Sachertorte are tasty and filling, so give them a try.
- **Learn a few German words:** Although many Austrians speak English, it's helpful to know some basic German phrases for communication.
- **Wear comfortable shoes:** Austria has plenty of cobblestone streets and hills, so comfortable shoes are a must.
- **Bring layers:** The weather in Austria can be unpredictable, so bring layers to adjust to changes in temperature.
- **Use public transportation:** Austria has a great public transportation system, including buses, trams, and trains, which are often cheaper and more convenient than driving.
- **Bring cash:** Some small businesses and markets may not accept credit cards, so bring cash for these situations.
- **Be respectful of customs and traditions:** Austrians take their customs and traditions seriously, so be respectful of them while visiting.
- **Check opening hours:** Many businesses and attractions may have limited hours or be closed on certain days, so check ahead of time to avoid disappointment.
- **Visit during the off-season:** Visiting Austria during the off-season (spring and fall) can be cheaper and less crowded.
- **Take a walking tour:** Many cities in Austria offer walking tours that can provide a great introduction to the history and culture of the area.

- **Visit the countryside:** Austria's countryside is stunning, so take a day trip outside the city to see it.
- **Attend a concert:** Austria is known for its classical music, so attending a concert can be a great experience.
- **Dress appropriately for attractions:** Many religious sites and formal attractions may require visitors to dress modestly, so be aware of the dress code.
- **Use a guidebook:** A guidebook can be a helpful resource for planning your trip and navigating your way around Austria.
- **Try the local wines:** Austria is home to many delicious wines, so try some while you're there.
- **Visit the Christmas markets:** Austria is famous for its Christmas markets, which are a great way to experience the festive atmosphere.
- **Check for discounts:** Many attractions offer discounts for students, seniors, and families, so check ahead of time to see if you qualify.
- **Don't forget travel insurance:** Travel insurance can provide peace of mind in case of any unexpected emergencies or accidents.
- **Be aware of pickpockets:** Like any tourist destination, Austria has its share of pickpockets, so be aware of your surroundings and keep your belongings close.
- **Enjoy the scenery:** Austria is a beautiful country with stunning scenery, so take the time to appreciate it while you're there.

Printed in Poland
by Amazon Fulfillment
Poland Sp. z o.o., Wrocław

40121377R00025